*Beatrix Potter's*

# BIRTHDAY BOOK

H.B.P.

*Beatrix Potter's*

# BIRTHDAY BOOK

COMPILED BY

ENID LINDER

FREDERICK WARNE

*Published by*

FREDERICK WARNE (Publishers) LTD: LONDON

FREDERICK WARNE & CO INC: NEW YORK



*Twelfth reprint 1983*

LIBRARY OF CONGRESS
CATALOG CARD NO. 73–89833

Standard Edition: ISBN 0 7232 1758 0
Leatherbound Edition: ISBN 0 7232 1815 3

*Printed and bound in Great Britain by*
*William Clowes (Beccles) Limited*
*Beccles and London*

D6911.1182

# INTRODUCTION

All seasons of the year are pictured in Beatrix Potter's books. Mother Hen with her family of chickens shops at Ginger & Pickles on a spring day. Tom Kitten and his two little sisters play in a summer garden where pansies, forget-me-nots and carnations bloom. Squirrel Nutkin and his friends gather their harvest in the autumn woods, and the Tailor of Gloucester shuffles home through the snow on winter nights after working all day on the Mayor's coat.

The pictures chosen for this little book have been arranged in such a way that those who write their names in it will be reminded by the illustrations not only of the season, but also of the month in which they were born.

# JANUARY

January 1

January 2

January 3

January 4
January 5
January 6
January 7

January 8
January 9
January 10
January 11

January 12

January 13

January 14

January 15

January 16

January 17

January 18

January 19

January 20

January 21

January 22

January 23

January 24

January 25

January 26

January 27

January 28

January 29

January 30

January 31

# FEBRUARY

February 1

February 2

February 3

February 4

February 5

February 6

February 7

February 8
February 9
February 10
February 11

February 12
February 13
February 14
February 15

February 16

February 17

"Then I will sing," replied Pig-wig. "You will not mind if I say iddy tidditty? I have forgotten some of the words."

February 18

February 19

February 20

February 21

Pussy-cat sits by the fire

February 22

Mom,

February 23

February 24

February 25

February 26
February 27
February 28
February 29

# MARCH

## March 1

## March 2

## March 3

March 4

March 5

March 6

March 7

March 8

March 9

March 10

March 11

March 12

March 13

March 14

March 15

March 16

March 17

March 18

March 19

March 20

March 21

March 22
March 23
March 24
March 25

March 26
March 27
March 28
March 29

March 30

March 31

The rain trickled down his
back, and for nearly an
hour he stared at the float.

# APRIL

## April 1

## April 2

## April 3

April 4

April 5

April 6

April 7

April 8

April 9

April 10

April 11

April 12

April 13

April 14

April 15

April 16

April 17

April 18

April 19

April 20

April 21

April 22

April 23

April 24

Heather Crockett
1973

April 25

We have a little garden,
  A garden of our own
And every day we water there
  The seeds that we have sown.

April 26
April 27
April 28
April 29

April 30

The eight little pigs had
very fine appetites.

# MAY

## May 1

## May 2

## May 3

May 4

Auntie Mary Gould.

May 5

May 6

May 7

May 8

May 9

May 10

May 11

"When the sun comes out again, you should see my garden and the flowers – roses and pinks and pansies"

May 12

May 13

May 14

May 15

May 16

May 17

May 18

May 19

May 20

Daddy,

May 21

May 22

May 23

May 24

May 25

Mr McGregor hung up
the little jacket and the
shoes for a scare-crow to
frighten the blackbirds.

May 26

May 27

May 28

May 29

A Uncle John

May 30

May 31

# JUNE

## June 1

## June 2

## June 3

June 4

June 5

June 6

June 7

June 8

June 9

June 10

June 11

June 12

June 13

June 14

Auntie Jill & van-de-Plass

June 15

## June 16

June 17

June 18

June 19

June 20

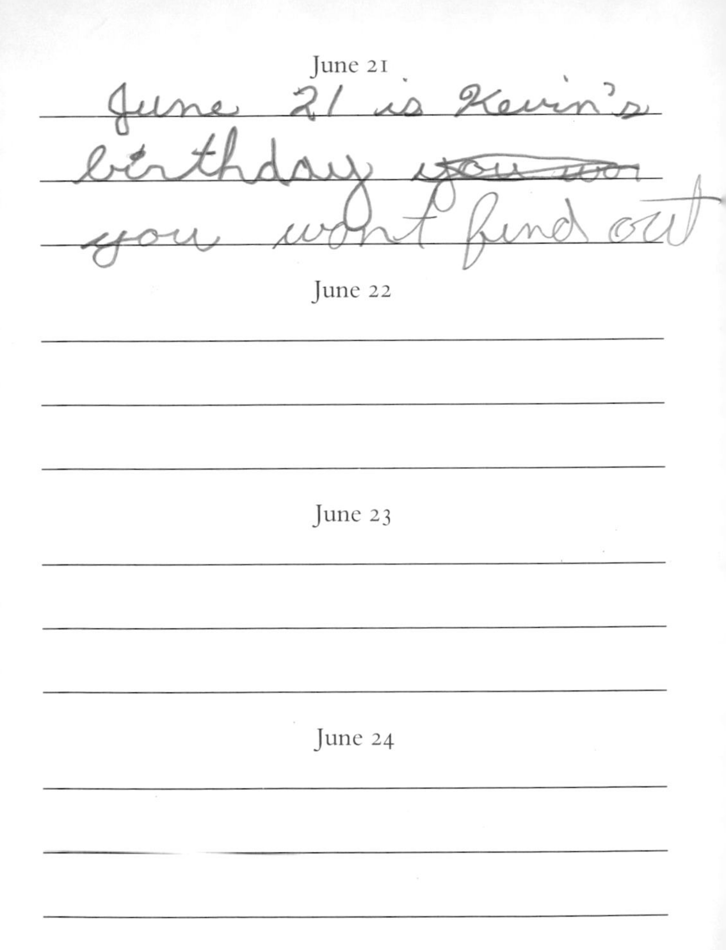

June 21

June 21 is Kevin's birthday ~~you won~~ you won't find out

June 22

June 23

June 24

June 25

June 26

June 27

June 28

June 29

June 30

# JULY

## July 1

## July 2

## July 3

July 4

July 5

July 6

July 7

July 8

July 9

July 10

July 11

July 12

July 13

July 14

July 15

July 16

July 17

## July 18

## July 19

## July 20

## July 21

After eating some peas
— Timmie Willie fell
fast asleep.

July 22

July 23

July 24

July 25

July 26

July 27

July 28

July 29

July 30

July 31

Karen - Joy Romkema

# AUGUST

## August 1

## August 2

## August 3

August 4

August 5

August 6

August 7

August 8
August 9
August 10
August 11

August 12

August 13

August 14

August 15

August 16
August 17
August 18
August 19

August 20

August 21

August 22

August 23

August 24

August 25

August 26
August 27
August 28
August 29

August 30

August 31

Flopsy, Mopsy, and Cotton-
tail who were good little
bunnies went down the lane to
gather blackberries

# SEPTEMBER

## September 1

## September 2

## September 3

September 4

September 5

September 6

September 7

September 8
September 9
September 10
September 11

September 12

September 13

September 14

September 15

September 16

September 17

September 18

September 19

September 20

September 21

September 22
September 23
September 24
September 25

September 26
September 27
September 28
September 29

## September 30

# OCTOBER

## October 1

## October 2

## October 3

October 4

October 5

October 6

October 7

October 8
October 9
October 10
October 11

October 12

October 13

October 14

October 15

October 16

October 17

October 18

October 19

October 20

October 21

October 22
October 23
October 24
October 25

October 26
October 27
October 28
October 29

October 30

October 31

# NOVEMBER

## November 1

## November 2

## November 3

November 4

November 5

Jennifer Anne

November 6

November 7

November 8

November 9

November 10

November 11

November 12
November 13
November 14
November 15

November 16

November 17

November 18
November 19
November 20
November 21

## November 22

## November 23

## November 24

## November 25

November 26
November 27
November 28
November 29

November 30

# DECEMBER

December 1

December 2

December 3

December 4

December 5

December 6

December 7

December 8
December 9
December 10
December 11

December 12

December 13

December 14

December 15

December 16

December 17

December 18

December 19

December 20

December 21

December 22

December 23

December 24

December 25

December 26
December 27
December 28
December 29

December 30

December 31

# SOURCES OF ILLUSTRATIONS